HEART SONGS:

MESSAGES FOR PARENTS
FROM CHILDREN ACROSS TIME

CHRISTINE LENICK

Heart Songs:

MESSAGES FOR PARENTS FROM CHILDREN ACROSS TIME

Copyright © 2001-2015 by Christine Lenick

All rights reserved. This book may not be reproduced in whole or in part, or transmitted in any form, or by any means electronic, mechanical, photocopying, recording, or other, without written permission from the publisher, except by a reviewer who may quote brief passages in a review.

Healing Arts Publishing
The Worldwide Center for the Healing Arts
P.O. Box 4223
Evergreen, CO 80437

ISBN: 978-0-9711522-7-4

OTHER HEALING ARTS PUBLISHING BOOKS

The Simple Truth About God
by Christine Lenick

La Simple Verdad Acerca de Dios
by Christine Lenick

Canciones del Corazón: Mensajes para Padres De los Niños a Través del Tiempo
by Christine Lenick

Healing Through Love
by Marilyn Innerfeld

HEALING ARTS PUBLISHING
EVERGREEN, CO

DEDICATION

I dedicate this book to the children of the world who seek only to express their joy and *be*. With a powerful choice to join the world, they come to teach and learn that we are each Perfect and Magnificent as God.

My life has been gifted with two special children, Tyler and Corey, who have joined my husband and me to experience the joy that we are as a family. My children are joyous, light-filled, communicative, inquisitive, hopeful, perfect, magnificent, and questing. It is with them that I learn each day about unconditional love. I thank them for choosing us.

Lastly, I thank my husband, Ben. Without his knowing heart, I may not have experienced my children. He knew he wanted a life filled with them. He has never let go of the pure joy of being one. He teaches all whom he meets how to experience joy and how to live.

With our hearts open we share this book with All.

CONTENTS

Preface	9
Introductory Letter	15
Heart Beat...	19
Who Children Are...	21
How Children Learn...	31
What Children Need...	43
Why Children Die...	53
How Children Live...	61
Being a Child...	71
Afterword	75
Acknowledgements	81
About The Author	83

PREFACE

Heart Songs: Messages for Parents from Children Across Time was flowed in January, 1999. One week earlier I flowed the book entitled, The Simple Truth About God. While different, both books share the powerful message that each of us is God. Simple, but challenging.

In October 1998 my life changed in extraordinary ways. Without seeking any change or spiritual enlightenment, I suddenly began to hear a voice, as though someone was dictating in my head. It was clear and true. The words were beautiful and breathtaking. Within a month, souls across time appeared to me, sharing amazing stories and universal lessons. I was moved by the messages and made time each day, after working as a consultant and caring for my children, to listen and journal the stories of those souls. At that time, I did so quite privately. After three months I had compiled a journal on everything from love and hate to abundance and lack.

During this time, my life path was shared as well. In this lifetime, my soul had one path as a messenger of the Truth that we are all God. I was to walk the earth sharing and teaching this simple but powerful Truth.

This was extraordinary because I had led a traditional life as a mother, wife, and businesswoman. I was neither religious, nor a spiritual seeker. But I was moved to tears by what I heard and felt from the souls and messages. With the knowing of my path I was faced with a powerful choice of whether or not to walk it. The messages made it clear that to do so would not be easy.

I was moved to honor this path because I recognized that in its simplicity, despite thousands of years of religious history, the message that each of us is God conveys all that is. I was only asked to be the messenger. I chose to honor my soul's path.

Within two weeks of acknowledging my choice to honor this path, I received a message that I was to write The Simple Truth About God. For seven days, working only at night, I flowed this extraordinary book, teaching each of us what it means to be

PREFACE

God. I cried, laughed, and learned with each word and the sharing of each soul. I will learn from this incredible work for the rest of my 'life. I am honored to share it.

One week later I received a message to write Heart Songs: Messages for Parents from Children Across Time. I was asked to write this book by a soul child named Eric. Eric had introduced himself to me in December, 1998 as my own child from another lifetime. I was stunned when I heard his words and felt his love. It was like a reunion that I never could have imagined. He told me that he is now the guardian of children that die and cross over into their spiritual experience. He wanted to write Heart Songs with me and brought forth each of the children's souls that spoke to me throughout this book.

The children who speak in Heart Songs seek to reach into your heart to awaken the knowing of your Truth. It is simple. To love your Self is the greatest gift of all. To share unconditional love with your child or the children in your life is the most powerful expression of Truth. Know that children will challenge you and test you, but know also that they are your Teachers.

Ask only, "What can I learn in this moment from these children who are so knowing?"

While this book is for parents, it shares powerful messages for everyone because we have each been a child and carry that child within us. This book gently caresses the reader to understand, through the eyes and hearts of children, what it means that we are each perfect as God. These children teach us the joy and exuberance that is of life.

My life was completely changed by my choice to live in Truth as God. I now live a nearly stress-free, joy-filled life that is beyond what I could ever have imagined possible. As my life changed, that of my family did as well. I began to be "with" my children rather than be "at" them. I recognized and honored how much they wanted to share time. As I let go of my fear, pain, and lack of selfLove, I allowed them to express their love for themselves.

This book will call on your heart to reawaken to the Truth that you are God, and thereby enable you to recognize that Truth in your children as well. With that awakening, you will be faced with

PREFACE

the choice in each moment to live in joy and celebration of your magnificence.

All will change the instant that you love your Self as perfect. Know that every moment is of great purpose, and choose to learn in joy-beyond-joy.

I share this and all that I am with an open heart.

Chris, Summer, 2001

INTRODUCTORY LETTER

Dear Friend,

I am a mother and parent in the lifetime I experience as now, like you. I have felt the joy and awe of watching my children as my own. I have felt blessed by the gift to my life that they are for they have taught me so much and will teach me so much more.

I have also felt the desire that they may grow up to be all that they can become. I have felt the "responsibility" to help them do so. I have tried to live up to that responsibility.

Now I realize that that "responsibility" is a fiction. We create it with our desire that they become the God-within that we are not. We do not understand it that way, but that is what is going on inside.

However, now I understand that we have it all backwards and are robbing our children of the very thing we want for them. As part of my spiritual journey – the journey of my soul in this lifetime – I have been asked to speak and share Truth. As a part of this role I have been asked by many children as soul energies across time to share their stories and messages so that others may learn.

How this sharing happens may be hard for you to understand. It is not necessary that you do so. It is only necessary, for the sake of your child as a soul across lifetimes, that you hear his or her message. It will be powerful.

It is necessary because children are the gateway to changing the world. They are the gateway because we are open to changing them. That openness allows us to learn that we do not need to change them, we can choose to learn from them. As a student, we only need to respect our Teachers and ask to learn.

The children and adults who share with you throughout this book do so because they are our Teachers. Honor them by listening to their message and learning how you can honor your children by parenting in a more powerful way.

INTRODUCTORY LETTER

I am honored to be the messenger. For you are here to learn, and it is your desire to learn that creates the opportunity for this book to have meaning. I am in awe of the soul energies that reach across time and through love so that they can reach us on the pages that follow.

This is for you and for them across time so that it may be for us as All.

Love,

Chris

HEART BEAT...

A child's heartbeat is the sound love makes. A child's heartbeat is what the doctor listens for to know the child is alive. A child's heartbeat is strong and quick. While a child's heartbeat slows down as a child grows older, a child's heart never stops beating. Even when a child dies as experienced in the physical, the sound of his or her heart does not.

Listen to the sound of your child's heart. Know that is the sound of love. Know that everything you do for and with your child in this lifetime either strengthens or diminishes that love. This book is about learning how we can all, as parents, strengthen that love in the lifetime we experience as together. It is all about love. Understanding love. Through this book and through your children you will also learn how to reawaken your love for yourself.

It is strange that we all believe that it is so much easier to share love with children than other adults.

We see the miracle of All in them. And yet, even with them, we so quickly stop loving them as the perfection that they are. Within moments of their birth we are looking for imperfections. We are contemplating how to help them be better. We forget instantly that they are perfect. Quickly, they become like us, for we teach them to be so. And, as they become so, the sounds of their heartbeats diminish.

This book is about relearning how to see children through God's eyes. It is about relearning how to see them as perfect. I am honored to be the messenger for many children who, with the guidance of my son Eric who has been reunited with me in this lifetime across time, will share with you their stories and teachings. You will come to know their wisdom and feel their desire for you to know it so that your children can too.

We will listen for the heartbeats of your children and know that you heard us.

-- *Eric and Chris*

WHO CHILDREN ARE...

Children are the soul in its essence and potential. The light in their eyes is the light from the soul fire. It burns so brightly at birth for the soul is in full connection with the knowledge of the God-within.

Children are in their perfection when they arrive into the physical being that will transport their soul through this lifetime. They have made a tremendous choice to be with you in a shared learning. Understand that it is no coincidence that your children are with you in this lifetime. They chose you.

It is funny how we often have it backwards. We think that our children are here because of us. Instead, we are here as parents because of them. Have you ever thanked your children for choosing to be with you? Have you thanked them for choosing to be here as your Teachers?

You and your children will learn from the experience of this lifetime but know fully that they are your Teachers. When you start to look at your children as your Teachers, you begin to honor and respect them rather than focus on getting them to respect you. As a matter of fact, as you begin to honor them as your Teachers you will find they will respect and honor you.

The energy of children is the energy of anxious souls returned to the earth desiring to live their soul journey. They have so much energy because they have not yet learned that their fire should not be so bright. It is bright because they come here filled with the knowledge of fully loving themselves. They know that God is One, God is All, They are God.

Children see the world through God's eyes. They see what they imagine as real. They see no obstacles to what they imagine as real - for by imagining it, it becomes real. We tell children that the imagination is not real, it is pretend. We tell them that pretending is what "children" do. We diminish the greatest gift children have – their ability to imagine their world in its greatest incarnation. Do not take this gift from your child.

WHO CHILDREN ARE...

Children do not see differences, they see all as One. Children embrace all in Joy! Their love is unconditional and has no bias. Learn from your children, for world peace may depend on it.

Know that children live with fully open hearts. They follow the joy and passion in their hearts in every one of their choices. They ask not whether something makes "sense" or is "right." They ask only whether it will give them joy.

We teach children to ignore their hearts and pay attention to their minds. How many times have you said to your child, "Have you thought about what you want?" or, "Think before you speak." Imagine instead saying to your child, "How do you feel about that?" or, "Tell me what your heart feels is the right thing to do." Imagine how much more self-confident children will feel when you tell them that if they follow their hearts everything they ever needed to know is inside them already.

Children remind us of pure joy -- a joy uninhibited by the illusions of the rules that bound our lives. Learn from them. Let go of your rules and follow your heart so that as you are in greater joy you will free your children to be as well.

A young girl, 3, with blonde hair in pigtails –

"My name is Sarah and I have been waiting for two days to speak with you."

Hi, Sarah. Thank you for waiting.

"I am mad at my Mom."

Why?

"My Mom beat me and my brother. We didn't do anything wrong. We would just be playing or something and my Mom would ask us a question. If we didn't answer right away she'd hit us. Finally, we decided together that we were going to leave so she couldn't hit us anymore. We decided to die."

How did you do that?

"Our love for one another decided. You see, every time my Mom hit my brother she was hitting me. We are and were one and the same. My Mom saw us as

different but we remembered what God[1] said -- we are all One. So one day as we were lying in the darkness our lights merged and decided it was enough. You know my brother and I had been together before and knew that we were choosing a Mom that had some hard lessons to learn. We thought we could help her and I think we did, even though it doesn't look that way. We let our Mom release us from that lifetime -- you call it killing. She is in jail now and thinks about us often. She is learning."

What do you want to teach us?

"Children choose, parents don't. We chose our mother. We knew how bothered she was. We chose to try to help her learn for we knew that we would learn about the absence of love -- the absence of selfLove. We learned how empty and dark it was. From my Mom's emptiness she sought to take our joy. Even in the saddest moments we knew that we could choose to leave. We had the power to choose.

---

[1] In the non-physical experience of Self we recognize all as God. References throughout the book to what God "said" are acknowledgments of learning from All. As God-As-All we experience others to experience all that we are. That experience is always one of equals.

You know, my Mom had that power, too. She just couldn't love herself enough to realize it. One day I told her I loved her and she hit me. She was in darkness.

Tell them to never hit their children. Tell them that they are hitting God and should think about that every moment. Tell them to love themselves so that they can teach their children to love themselves. Tell them! Tell them!

Thank you for listening! Thank you for sharing my message."

A boy, about 8, dressed very formally –

"I am James. Eric told me to talk to you about my life. I lived with a very rich family. I chose to live with them because I thought if I had lots of money that I'd never be unhappy. Boy, was I wrong.

My parents worried more about how I was then who I was. They worried about how I looked and acted, but not what I felt. They worried more about what others thought about me as them than what I thought about me as me. My parents never asked me what I felt or who I was. I don't really think they cared. You know, when

WHO CHILDREN ARE...

I was first born, I had this light inside me. At first, I felt this tremendous love from my parents. But after awhile I felt like I was a doll they were dressing up to show others. My light started to go out and I tried to keep it going but couldn't. Finally, I left."

How did you do that?

"I let my body get sick, real sick. I let it die. My parents cried. They put me in those fancy clothes and buried me."

What do you want to teach us?

"To care. Tell them to care about how their children feel. Tell them to care about what makes their child joyous. Tell them to watch the light inside and to keep it burning by caring about what their children care about. Tell them that if they care about what their children care about, their children's flames will burn brightly. Tell them to care. Thank you. Eric was right, you will listen."

Thanks.

A baby in utero –

"I do not have a name. Not yet. I have a family, though. I am waiting to be born."

Has your soul entered the physical body of the developing baby?

"Well, I come and go. I have chosen my family and they are getting my body ready for me. I do not need to be there yet but I like to visit. I am getting ready, too, you know. You see, I have waited a long time to find a new family. I needed to find one that could teach me about love – selfLove. And I found one. There aren't too many of those kinds of families so I had to wait a long time. It is finally my turn. So right now I spend some time with God[2]* and some time with my new family by visiting my body."

What do you want to teach us?

"The body is really the least important part. Children choose families so that their souls can learn. The most important part is how we will help one another learn.

---

2 In the non-physical experience of Self we interact with All as God. We recognize the other as Self as we are as God.

WHO CHILDREN ARE...

Families focus so much attention and time on the body. They want to make sure everything is there, then that everything works right, and then that everything works according to some kind of plan. My new Mom, though, she understands that this is backwards. I've watched her with my brothers and sisters. She focuses on asking what we need to learn, how she can help us do so, and what makes our fire burn so brightly. She asks us why we chose her and honors the importance of being both teacher and student.

Tell them that it is never too early to begin asking their children these questions. Tell them that even if they speak to their unborn children, that energy will reach them. It doesn't matter if their energy is not inside their body. Tell them I am going to have a great life. Thanks for sharing this. Tell them to watch for me."

How will we know who you are?

Tell them that I will be in the park and my Mom will be asking me what would give me the most joy today? Tell them I'll wave to them. Thanks."

HOW CHILDREN LEARN...

Children do not learn in school, they learn in life. School is but one small part of life. Life, as you see it as a lifetime, is but one small part of many lifetimes. Children learn across lifetimes and sometimes in many lifetimes at once.

This concept is hard to understand when you view time as linear. Know that it is unimportant that you understand that time is not linear. It is important that you understand how learning is multi-dimensional. The child who asks you a peculiar question in this lifetime is probably just building on an understanding gained either in a different lifetime or in a different experience of Self.

What is important is that you stop focusing on skills. By focusing so strongly on skills like reading, writing, math, and science we teach children that which is important is outside of them. Children will naturally seek to understand these "things" when we help them learn about themselves.

Instead, spend some of the time you are now focusing on skills teaching your children how to love themselves, celebrating their uniqueness, and honoring them. Talk to your children about the power of selfLove, for it is all-powerful. If you want your children to be self-confident and strong, have them say "I love me, I love the God-within that I am, I love God" everyday.

Plan a party or parties to celebrate your child's unique traits. Children will begin to develop pride in themselves for their perfection if you celebrate that perfection. Stop celebrating age. Celebrate "being."

Finally, teach your children to honor and show gratitude to their souls for the incredible journey it is on across time. Imagine how you will expand their sense of self and their role in following their hearts by making life choices that will honor their soul's purpose in this lifetime. Everyday, tell them to close their eyes and see the fire inside them. Tell them the fire is their soul's energy living its passion. But teach them that they are their soul's firekeeper and the firekeeper must tend and nurture the fire. Tell them to thank their souls everyday for this wonderful journey of learning in joy. Tell them! Tell them!

Teach them that learning is about Life. Every choice and every thought they have in life creates an energy through which they will learn. Teach them that their lives are a masterpiece and every brushstroke they make will teach them and honor them if they but ask to learn.

Teach them to love themselves. Teach them how to celebrate themselves. Teach them to be the firekeepers. Teach them about the power of their thoughts and choices. Then honor them and watch how they will learn.

A young shy boy, 2 –

Who are you?

"I am Sampson. My Mom and Dad called me Sam. I left my Mom and Dad so that they could learn about death. I didn't leave so much as I had agreed to leave

before I went there, so it was time. I had an accident. My Mom feels bad, real bad, but she is learning from this. You know my Mom is a scientist. She's famous. My Dad is a professor. He reads a lot. They wanted me to be smart like they were. Things didn't work out that way though because everything they learned in books did not prepare them for this, my leaving. My Mom is now reading about Death. She wants to understand what happened. What she will discover is that she will learn more about herself than me. She will learn how to learn from herself and how to consult her heart. She will begin to see books as more of something extra than everything.

My Dad, well, he is learning too. He's learning how to be with his sadness and how to be with my Mom. He thinks he understands Death but really he doesn't because he doesn't understand Life. He will learn how to live his Life because he will learn that Life is but a moment.

You know, I learned too from my lifetime. I wasn't even there long but I learned about how people hide from their hearts. They hide in their books and their work. I learned how empty that can be. I was the light for my Mom and Dad. I filled that emptiness and called them out of their books. But I couldn't be their light; they must be that for themselves.

I left. We all learned. Isn't that perfect? I gotta go now. Thanks.

Tell them Sam said hi!"

A little African boy named Eshon –

"I am Eshon, son of the leader of the Woozon. We live in the jungle and live off of the jungle. We are natives of the jungle and seek no contact with your world. I come to you spiritually because you are teaching the most important of lessons – how to let children learn. For learning is the key to Life for it is all of Life. Watch your children. There is not a moment from their birth to their death – yes, they are always your children – that they are not learning about themselves and their world. In the jungle all of Life is learning, for with our people the greatest honor is to share with another something one has learned about himself. I shared my learning about the inner fire with my father and grandfather yesterday. I taught them how to feel their fire for theirs are dim with time and neglect.

There are few places like the jungle left that honor all Life as learning. Your schools and houses of worship have stolen this Truth from you. They have reduced learning to a requirement rather than an expression of the heart in passion for the soul. There is time for many that have not yet unlearned the joy of their soul seeking to learn in every moment.

Tell them to pretend that life is a jungle. The jungle is wild, mysterious and free. Their Life is wild, mysterious, and free. Tell them to roam in the jungle, watch for the amazing animals, and seek out Life's mysteries. Tell them that their Life is the jungle. Honor themselves for what they learn by sharing it so that it will honor them.

Thanks for your work."

A girl named Melissa with short brown hair in a wheelchair –

"I'm Melissa. I have no legs. Well, I have them, they just don't work so it is as if I do not have them. Don't feel sorry or bad for me. I'm going to dance someday because that is what I am going to learn to do. I just

haven't found anyone who can teach me yet. Maybe I will teach myself and then teach others.

I have this friend at the hospital who hurt his head. He can't talk right anymore. Someone is trying to teach him how to talk all over. You know what he told me?"

What?

"He told me that his accident taught him how we all talk too much and need to listen. He told me he wants to learn to be the world's best listener. He will be because that is what he wants to learn about. He said he is going to listen to me dance someday. He will."

What do you most want to teach us?

"That learning is about desire, not need. I don't need to learn how to dance. I want to. My friend doesn't need to learn how to listen. As a matter of fact, most think he needs to learn how to talk. He has no interest in talking, but boy does he want to learn how to listen.

Ask yourself and your children what they "want" to learn about? Then help them learn about that. When the "that" changes, change with them. Do not worry about what you think they need, they know. Remember that this is one small lifetime so don't waste it on stuff you think they need. They know, just ask them.

Thanks for listening to me. My friend would like you because you listen. See ya."

A baby boy in his Mom's arms, sleeping –

"Listen...listen. I have to whisper because my Mom wants me to be sleeping. I'm not tired so I'm kind of resting here. I wanted to tell you something."

What?

"Before I came here I found out what I am going to learn. When I got here everyone around me started to joke and say what I was going to do in my life. They said I was going to be like my Dad and go to his prep school and college. I like my Dad, but that's not what I want to do here. So I've been thinking."

About what?

"How to live my own life. You see, I'm here to learn about Joy. I'm here to learn about how to live my life in Joy. When I'm little I think that will be easy. But when I get a

little bigger, then I have my work cut out for me. Not too many kids I see are living in Joy when they get older. No one lets them. Most give up and kind of give in to the rules because they don't want to disappoint their parents. Boy, would their parents be disappointed if they knew what their kids were giving up on. You know, they are giving up on themselves. Well, I won't do that."

What do you want to teach us?

"Tell your children to live their lives. It is their life. Tell everyone to stop telling them what their life should be. Whose life is it anyway? It is odd how parents who have given up their own lives so quickly take their children's lives. Somehow it makes what they did less painful.

Well, it is painful. See your children's lives as much more expansive and purposeful than you do. Then ask them to teach you about their grandest vision for their lives. Tell them this vision can and will change as they grow older but that they should never stop learning what they need to learn to live that vision. Never tell them it is too grand. Never. I'm not going to prep school, by the way. Take care."

A teenage girl who can't talk but uses sign language –

"My name is Helen. You know me."

You are Helen Keller.

"Yes. You honored me with your love for my poem. I thank you. Now I am here to teach you about learning. All I ever did was learn. Nothing I had worked right to help me learn but I just kept on learning. Do you know how I learned?"

How?

"I learned with my heart. I could feel everything, and you know what? So can your children. You need not say a word or show them a thing. Let them feel your energy through their heart and they will learn. They will learn about love, about caring, about listening, about feeling, about honoring. They will learn everything they need to know through their heart.

Everyone thought my life was spectacular even though they felt sorry for me. Little did they know that what they couldn't see was even more spectacular.

Tell everyone that what they can't see is spectacular! Tell them to teach their children to love themselves just as they are for they are perfect. Tell them to visit their heart everyday and to surround it with love. Tell them to listen with their heart and they will know all the answers they need to know. Tell them it is spectacular.

I love you with my heart. Thank you."

WHAT CHILDREN NEED...

Children need Love. Why is it so hard for you to give this simple gift to your children? Children need nothing else and yet you focus so much time and effort on what is least important. You hide behind the illusion that the other is important because you find it so hard to love them.

Don't object. The way you love them is not Love. It is not unconditional. It is conditional. By sharing this kind of love you rob your children of their souls. You do not give them love so much as take away from their love of Self. Do you not understand how harmful this is?

You do not mean to do this, but you must now stop. You must come to terms with your own lack of selfLove so that you can choose to love your children as you need to be loved – unconditionally. Start by saying "I love me" one hundred times every day. Slowly you will find it easier to tell your children you love them. After that you will find it easier to love them just as they are, for they are perfect.

Stop focusing on what you think they need to be better. Stop focusing on what you perceive they would need to be perfect. Your perception is actually creating a need that was not there.

See your children living across the lifetimes that they do. Know that they have everything they need inside them for the learning they will do in this lifetime. They only need to know that, and they will know by loving themselves.

Tell them that you love them just as they are, for they are perfect. Tell them to say "I love me, I love the God-within that I am" every day. Teach them that they have all the answers inside, and in teaching them this they will "need" less and have more.

Celebrate your children! They are perfect! As you celebrate them you will be celebrating you, too, for you are perfect.

A severely deformed little boy, 3 or 4, named Josh ...

"I am Josh. I look funny and I feel funny looking. Everyone stares at me. I stare at myself because what they see is not me. I am beginning to see what they see and it makes me sad. I didn't used to see that. I used to see my light. It was bright white. It was strong. I loved it everyday. It's not so bright anymore."

Josh, what do you most want to teach us?

"All I needed was Love. Nobody could see their way to giving me that. Nobody. They saw their way to saying, "I love you but maybe we can get your face fixed . . . maybe there will be a miracle." They never loved me; they only loved the me they thought I could be with help.

I loved me when I got here. God[3]* loved me and taught me to love me. But that isn't enough because I learned from everyone around me. My Grandmother even said she couldn't stand to look at me. When I heard her

---

3 In the non-physical experience of Self we recognize All as God. References throughout the book to "God's love" and how we learn refer to our experience of All as love for Self. SelfLove allows all-knowing.

say that I remember taking a good look at myself and realizing she was right. I didn't look like them. I stopped loving me.

Tell them not to see so powerfully with their eyes. See with their hearts because all on the earth plane are God. The way they look has nothing to do with it. The only thing anyone needs is to be loved just as they are, for they are perfect.

Don't feel sorry for me. Your pity is not love. It is pity. It says I am less than you are or less than perfect. Look at me as perfection, for I am. I chose this lifetime for it is just another way to experience perfection and learn about the God-within.

What have you chosen and what have your children chosen? See them with your heart. For as you open the eyes of your heart you will see the miracle that we all are – you will truly begin to see.

Thank you. I feel better."

I love you.

Josh is still there . . .

"Can you tell my Mom that it is okay that she could never look at me? Tell her to love herself for we both learned. Tell her I found peace when I left because it hurt too much to live without love. There is lots of love here. Tell her I'm happy."

Annette – tall girl of 11 or 12 –

"Hi! Guess what I have? I have everything; but what I want most? Time. I have toys, games, friends, clothes and stuff. But I don't have time with my parents. My Dad travels a lot, and when he is here he's never here. You know, he's watching football or working outside. He's always busy. Mom, she's here more because she doesn't have to travel for her job, but when she gets home she's always busy getting us ready for something – softball or piano or homework. She never just sits down with us. Then it turns out we don't have enough time to be together. You know what?"

What?

I love my Mom and Dad but I say it a lot less lately. They say it a lot less to me, too. I understand that they have to work but what about when they aren't working? Sometimes I get the feeling that I'm just not as important as "stuff."

Well, can you tell them that nothing is important but time? Time for being together and sharing love. Tell them to stop signing up for things and running everywhere. Who cares? Tell them everything they need to do with their children they can do at home. Everything. They just need to realize that and they will see how much there is to do together at home. Tell them to stop, please."

Thank you for sharing.

"You're welcome."

A group of children, multicultural, very cheerful . . .

Who are you? . . . Don't all yell at once.

"I'm Aisha, I'm Devon, I'm Sunam, I'm Deion, I'm Selop, I'm Susan , I'm Kirk- they call me Captain Kirk . . . !"

Captain Kirk, what do you want to teach us?

"Well, we have been working on a song about children and we want to sing it."

WHAT CHILDREN NEED...

Should I write it down?

"Yes. We will go slowly. Ready?"

Yes.

"Children are the gifts of God.

Children are the gifts of a Lifetime.

We are the children of the world and we are the gift to the world.

Fill us not with your sadness and hate. Fill us not with your concern.

Fill us with love for ourselves, for we are the gift to the world.

Fill us; fill our hearts for when we arrive we are all filled with the brightest of lights.

Our fire is your fire, for we are living into the you that has lived.

Give us not the burdens of your thoughts. Give us not the fears for yourself. Give us not less than we are.

Give us only your love for us in our perfection. Love us! Love us! Love us! For we so love you just as you are.

We are the miracle and the gift to the world. Love us!"

"Yeah!!!! Yeah!!!" The children are running around delighted.

"Do you like it?"

I love it. They will love it too. Thank you. It is fantastic.

"Great. We have to go now. Bye."

A six-year-old boy whose brain is deformed.

They want to take his brain out and they are afraid he will die . . .

"They want to take my brain out. I can't live without a brain . . . well, sort of . . . . Well, not in their world, at least. Why are they trying to "kill" me just because my brain isn't shaped right and doesn't do everything on time. Who cares? What's the rush anyway? I'm afraid.

WHAT CHILDREN NEED...

You know what? The doctor told my Mom and Dad that this surgery is experimental. How can they make me an experiment? Why can't they experiment on loving me and see how I do? You know what, I'd do better than this surgery. Why are they making it so hard?"

What do you want to teach us?

"Tell them my brain doesn't matter and neither does theirs. It is the fire inside them that matters, and everyone they know helps them fuel it. When their parents don't teach them to love themselves, the fire begins to diminish. When the parents don't love them it can barely stay alive. When everyone around them doesn't love them the fire will go out.

Tell them Love – unconditional Love – is the most powerful thing on earth. Look into the eyes of your children and tell them that you love them with the love of the universe just the way they are.

Tell my Mom and Dad to tell me. Please . . . ."

What's your name?

"My name is Jack – funny Jack."

Jack and I worked together to tell his parents. Thank you Jack. All is all right now.

"I feel the light, it is so bright. Thank you."

WHY CHILDREN DIE...

Children do not die. Children dance across lifetimes. The dance is the soul's movement in joy with itself. What you perceive as death is the soul's release from one lifetime into the moment that is preparation for another.

Why do you put so much energy into Death as a finite event marking a tragedy? Yes, you feel tremendous loss and pain, but that is only because you choose to do so. Can you not as easily honor the sadness because you will not be able to hold your child, but then, move into a new kind of relationship with your child's soul? Can you not be forever in love and thanks with your child's soul for sharing as your Teacher with you in this lifetime?

Know that you will be with your child again. Your child is your Teacher and even now, if you have lost a child, as you search for answers, your child is with you in love on your journey. You will be reunited with your Teacher, for you have a bond that unites you across lifetimes.

Know also that love is a forever bond -- forever through time and across time. You can access that tremendous love you feel across time in order to be with your child in the moment you are experiencing as now. There are no limits. Know this to be true, and follow your heart.

Recognize that children die for a reason, sometimes for their parents. Children, as Teachers, teach through both pain and joy; it is you as the parent who seeks to see them only in joy. Honor their lesson and the choice that you both made about how that lesson would occur. That choice was part of your bond. Know that when your child left, it was time. They were just honoring their choice, made prior to birth, to teach you and others through their early physical death.

Finally, know that when children die they are never alone. Never. Children are met by members of their soul family as they cross through our veiled worlds. They are guided to a place where they learn their

WHY CHILDREN DIE...

life's lesson and they are with God-As-All.[4*] Children are then taken to meet with advanced and troubled souls for both learning and teaching. They learn Universal truths that advance their souls. When the time is right, children's souls come back so that their soul continues its learning.

Let your child go with love and thanks if they have left you. Honor them as they have honored you. Go on with your life so that they can go on with theirs.

A young African American boy, 3, named Esau –

"I am Esau. I died yesterday. Everything happened so fast. Now I am here with everyone I know from a long time ago. I didn't want to leave, but I had to because my Dad must learn about loss and faith. Loss is an illusion and faith is in oneself. This will be hard for my Dad but it is important that he learns. Dad will thank me some day."

---

4 We are never alone except in judgment of our Self. Children, upon death, experience no moment of judgment. So children are never alone. We are always All that we are for God-within is God-As-All. The love that bonds us with others in our physical lifetime is with us across time unless we choose otherwise.

What do you most want to teach us?

"Tell everyone that it is a big coming and going. There are souls like me coming and going all the time. Here I get to understand everything and know God's[5] love as I am. There I got to understand how hard we make it to live God's love as oneself.

You know every soul that leaves here is convinced that this time they will live fully as the God-within that they are. If only everyone there understood how easy it is to do that, and let them, the world would be different. All you need to do is tell them they are perfect and love them unconditionally. Through your love and acceptance they will love themselves.

Understand that some, even when loved unconditionally, must go, for their time is up. They have learned and must teach. Say goodbye and get on with your life. For if you do not they cannot get on with theirs.

Thanks for sharing this message."

---

5 In the non-physical experience of Self we recognize All as God. References throughout the book to "God's love" and how we learn refer to our experience of All as love for Self.

A little girl with glasses, Allison, 6 -

"Hi! I love you. We all want to talk with you because we are so misunderstood. Everyone thinks that children shouldn't die and that it is so horrible when it happens. Yes, it is sad, but it is not horrible.

The only reason it is sad is that children are perceived as more vulnerable. It is as if we do not understand what is going on. You know what? We understand just as well and sometimes better than adults do. Adults who have not honored the God-within that they are have lost their connection to God-As-All.[6]* For us, we are closer to it because we just got here. And you know, we are equal to our parents spiritually. It is only a question of awareness, and many, if not most of us, are more aware."

What do you most want to teach us?

"Focus on Life, not Death. Put no energy to Death for it is but a blink of an eye that changes the cast of your Life. Your Life is still full of Teachers and learning.

---

[6] To honor our Self as God with love and acceptance is to know who we are. To celebrate that Truth with joy is to *live*.

Understand that this is so. One of your Teachers has gifted you with the ultimate lesson if you are ready for it -- Oneness. Step back and realize that you are One with your child always, forever, and in the now that you are experiencing. It is not a leaving, it is a becoming.

Please share this lesson. Be One with all of us, for we are One with you. Thank you."

A tall handsome young man, 18, named Derek –

"I lost my brother. He drowned. It was an accident. It shouldn't have happened. We have all always missed him. My Mom and Dad have never stopped missing him. We loved him.

My brother speaks to me sometimes. He tells me that love never ends and that he feels our love all the time. He tells me that someday we will be together again because he's not alone there.

I tell him we miss him and he says we should celebrate his death because it wasn't a death, it was a birth. He says he got to learn about life and be with God-

As-All.[7]* *He says that he is in a joyous place and is learning a lot. He told me that Mom and Dad have to go on with their lives. He says that as long as they are really sad and think his death was the end of their lives, it will be. It wasn't.*

They just have convinced themselves so.

My brother told me that souls can't move on until those that were connected to them let them go. He wants me to tell my parents so that he can move on. He wants to move on. Can you tell them?"

Yes. How?

"Write this book and I'll get them one."

Okay.

"Thanks. I'll tell my brother that you are helping us."

An old woman with white hair named No Eyes –

"I cannot see as you see, but I see more. I am No Eyes, the Indian woman of the mountains. We have met.

---

7 Upon death, we are with All that we are -- God-As-All.

This is important and that is why I have come to you.

These children that you speak with have not died. For no one dies, they merely change parts in the play. Focus not on their absence. Focus on the play. They have played their part and now you must play yours. Honor them as they have honored you.

Know that honoring them means to thank them for dying, as you perceive their leaving. Thank them, for they left so that you may learn and live.

They are the greatest Teachers. These children share wisdom that you have buried in your experience of yourself across lifetimes. They share it because you had not yet taught them not to do so. They share it because it is of their heart.

Know that you will have others and be others. As you learn from them you prepare yourself to be them again. Your time will come and you will remember this gift -- for it is a gift of life, not death.

Thank them and they will thank you."

HOW CHILDREN LIVE...

Children live as fully in every moment as the first and last moment that it is. Learn from them. They live in joy, abundance, and love. They live fully.

They know that they do not need more. Do not tell them that they do, for then they will need more. Know that when you tell your child that they are perfect, you tell them to continue to live fully. It is freeing. Let them be free.

You are their student. Honor that relationship and learn from them about how to live. Find joy in your imagination as you create your world. For if you think it, it will be.

Dance from the mountaintops! Laugh at yourself and the sun! Play in the flowers! Break the rules! Live!

Children see with God's eyes as All. You should, too. For now, one of the few things you do see with God's eyes is the perfection of a newborn baby. See your world as the perfection that it is. Know that you are perfect and so are your children.

Take time each day just to be. Children take time when they are little and then we teach them that that is a waste of time. Time that is not honored with fullness is a waste of time.

Children love unconditionally. Their love has no bounds. Teach them how to love themselves and you will watch their love grow. Learn from them, and you will watch yours grow.

Children live fully for they know no other way. Tell them that they are perfect, and they will ask you to live fully, too.

A very excited young boy who is yelling –

"Listen to me! I am me!!!! Do you know how good that feels? It is so freeing to be me. I love me. That is even more freeing. I know what I need, for I am perfectly me. Yippee!! Yippee!!

HOW CHILDREN LIVE...

What do you most want to teach us?

"How wonderful you are, and how wonderful your children are. Why can you not accept that? What stops you even for an instant? Whatever it is, it is not the Truth. The only Truth is that you are perfect as the God-within that you are. Nothing else matters.

Give your children your unconditional love for them in their perfection. God-As-All[8]* told me that I am perfect when I got here because I had no flame left. I had lost the light of selfLove. My Mom and Dad thought I had to be something else, and I kept feeling like less until it was dark inside.

Listen; tell your children now. As you tell them you will watch them dance in joy. You should tell yourself, too, so that you can dance in joy with them. Now that will be living. Thanks."

---

8 Upon death we experience the purity of our Truth -- that we are perfect and magnificent as God. In our non-physical experience of Self we know Acceptance from All that we are - God-As-All.

A young shy girl named Marilyn –

"You know me now. I am your friend. I didn't know you then; but I am here with you now, as your friend from then, so that I can teach others what I have learned. I didn't live fully. My Mommy and Daddy didn't let me. It was quiet and it hurt sometimes. I lived by myself a lot so I wouldn't bother anyone or attract their attention or wrath. I didn't live. I stayed quiet.

You know me now. Now I am living. I love you for that as my friend."

What do you most want to teach us?

"Tell the children that no one can ever take away their love of Self. It is a fire inside them, and they are the firekeeper. Tell them to fuel it everyday, no matter what anyone says or no matter how anyone makes them feel. Tell them to know that I love them with my love for all as One.

You know, when I was little I knew inside that I was special even though the world outside told me I wasn't. I was right. Tell the children that what they "know" is right, for it is in their perfection.

Tell the parents that to steal a child's soul is a grave undertaking. For the soul has a journey that will outlast the theft. Tell them that they are really stealing their soul's joy with such self-hate that they would hurt another. There is another way.

Tell them to love themselves. Tell them to say "I love me, I am God, and I love the God-within that I am." Tell them I love them. Thanks, Friend."

An old man in his nineties –

"I am very old. I ought to have died already but I'm not ready. It took me a long time to understand how to live my life fully. I had to learn to live each moment as my first and last. I had to learn to live them fully.

For a long time I watched children. I sat in the park and watched them run and play. I watched them find amusement in dirt and joy in the wind. I listened to their sounds, for they are the sounds of feelings, not thoughts. I sat on my bench and every once in awhile a little one would sit there, too. They always said "hi" with their heart open.

I sat on that bench after having lived a full life. I had worked and married. I had children and then had grandchildren. But I had not understood what living is until I sat and watched children.

Parents don't see it. For the parents didn't sit and watch, they watched out for. Tell them to sit and watch. There is really little to watch out for. Their children will be okay. Tell them to learn as I did how to live fully. Only children know this secret.

I know now that living fully is being in one's love for oneself. It is celebrating that love by enjoying everything and every way one interacts with the world, even the dirt. It is living just that moment with joy and openness.

Now I sit here by this window. I cannot get to the park anymore, but you know what? I am there. Even here in this chair I play with each moment, I dance with the raindrops, I run naked in the moonlight. This is fantastic, and I owe it all to the children in the park. Thank them for me, okay?"

Yes. Thank you.

A Mother, middle aged, who died suddenly leaving her children, James, Alison, and Eric –

"Dear Friends. I come to you now with the plea that you realize what an enormous impact you have on your children. Every thought and desire you have for them as their parent calls out in them the creation of that energy. If you fear for their health or think they will have trouble making friends, then they will be sickly or lonely. Your energy is so strong because they are connected to you across time in love. Had I only known."

What do you most want to teach us?

"I want you to love them unconditionally so that you can watch them fully be who they are -- God. Do not for a second think they need to be different. Yes, I know they need to be taught the social graces of our world, but know that that is different from teaching them they do not have everything inside them. See them as perfect, not imperfect. Do not compare them to others, for each is unique with gifts that no other has in the universe. Think about how powerful that is, and see your role as helping them see and celebrate

that uniqueness. You have no other role. That is it. Let everything else go.

I wish I had known this then. At least I know it now for my next lifetime. I cannot wait to celebrate my children to come. I celebrate those I left behind now with the knowing that I am touching their souls and refueling their fires. Time is forever and a moment. Start now to do only that small part you are called upon to do.

Thank you for this work. It will touch many."

A baby being born ---

"Wow! I made it. That last part was tough. Wait, I need to cry so that they will put me down. Okay. This is fantastic! I can't believe it. I have been waiting a long time to be here and I made it. Yippee! Yippee! You have to understand that getting back here takes time sometimes. I had to wait so that I could really learn my last lesson. Finally, they said I was ready to go. I love it here. It is a challenge here because no one tells you how to love yourself and instead they tell you they are worried about this or that. This time I'm just not going to listen. You watch me."

What do you most want to teach us?

"All is to be celebrated. Start dancing and stop preparing. Hey, time is forever and just a day. What are you preparing for? You are perfect and so are your children. There is nothing to do except enjoy what you most enjoy. Be together with your children -- just be. It is not about "becoming." It is about "being." Even your baby, like me, is just to be enjoyed. Stop watching to see when your baby will do this or that. You end up missing what they are doing now. Now is all that matters. Then will matter when it is now.

Well, I've gotta go. I am so excited. Wow!"

BEING A CHILD…

Being a child is like being the sun. Your spirit rises up each day in command of the world. You are strong, hopeful, and confident. You are just who you are.

Being a child is to be vulnerable to those who have lost the spirit of the sun. They are the dark clouds who steal your light and muffle your warmth.

Being a child is being the beginning and end. It is being.

Be like your child. Become the you that is the sun. Let your light shine forth in command of your world. For as you become your child, you become a parent. A parent is a steward or guide. You, in your celebration of Self, guide your child to his or her celebration of Self.

Know that you are to do nothing else but celebrate the uniqueness of your child or children. See that uniqueness like a culture that is to be explored and enjoyed. Partake in the joy of your children, for if you do not you will find they will grow up joyless.

This is a shared journey across time for you and your child. You choose how it will be. Be the child you are, and be with them as the children they are. It will be more joyous than you imagine!

It is Eric...

"Mom, it is me. We have done well, but I want to share one more thing. Mom, it is so easy but so many make it so hard. I know they will ask you why children have to suffer sometimes if they are the sun? Suffering is but another teacher. Perfection does not mean the absence of pain; it means the absence of self-doubt. One can be fully in understanding of who they are and the purpose of their journey on earth, and they can choose pain. Children sometimes choose pain and sometimes are told to feel it.

This book is about teaching you, as a parent, to let your child choose. For once you recognize that you can call forth pain, then you can stop doing so. Once you recognize that children can choose pain, you can teach them that they can choose health.

BEING A CHILD...

Being a child is a wondrous and scary experience. It is wondrous if one looks with God's eyes, but it is scary when one looks through the eyes of self-doubt. Being a child is short-lived for most, but across time for the lucky few. Know that we are always children seeking to be in that total selfLove as God-within. Love yourself as God-within and be the child you are, now and forever.

Thank you for listening. We all thank you."

AFTERWORD

Many readers of this book and The Simple Truth About God have asked me whether I often speak with "souls" like Eric. The answer is "no." Sometimes Eric will contact me if it is important that I either help a child or he needs my help. I have the ability to work across time, and so I do when it will serve the need of the one who so seeks the guidance.

Most often I work with the essences or souls of children and adults in our present physical experience either guiding them with messages from their hearts or sharing healing energy.

Parents should be aware that until the age of thirteen parents and their children are co-creators. Every word and thought of the parent creates on behalf of the child. Until a child reaches age thirteen, parents can give permission for "energy guides" to work with their children without the child's conscious participation. This choice, however, should not be made lightly.

As a general rule, energy work should not be done on children under the age of five more than twice during those early years. Children's energy or essences are very pure and quite sensitive. After age five, energetic work should only'lpp be used when necessary. Parents should know that all healing modalities, medical and non-traditional or alternative, are equal. All must be honored so that the child can heal easily as they so choose.

It is valuable to understand that children who are seriously ill during the first twelve years of life made that choice prior to incarnation in their physical bodies. They did so in order to teach their parents and families. Understanding this truth is important because the willingness of the parent and family to acknowledge that the lesson is theirs impacts the healing of the child and family. Many parents seek only to "heal" their child and do not recognize that they too must heal. The child is gifting them with this opportunity and lesson.

I am honored to share my Self with the children who choose to know me.

AFTERWORD

Message From Eric

During the summer of 2001, as I prepared this manuscript for publication, I came into the knowing that Eric wanted to share an additional message with readers. It is a powerful one. I share it with love.

"My dearest readers, I have much to share with you. These pages share but a fraction of the words of children who seek to reach into the hearts of All so that we can be all that we are in joy.

I am one like you who chose to enjoy the experience of a physical lifetime many times. One time most closely with Chris as my mother. It was short but exquisite, for she is a special Being.

I have decided, however, to remain in my purest experience of Self so that I can act as a guardian of all children who cross over from their physical experience. It is a choice of joy.

Parents must know one thing. The children I meet are often grieving, for not only have they left those they loved at such an early age of experience, but more so because they were not heard. They were treated as "children" and not spiritual equals with great knowing. They were silenced by many around them who were in great judgment and self-hatred.

I speak these words not to alarm you, but instead to say, "Wake Up!" These are not children, but God. Why is it so hard for you to see that? Why do you look at them and "hope" that they will be "well" or "turn out okay?" Why do you pity those who have chosen paths with greater challenge? Why?

Stop judging from your eyes of pain and experience their Perfection. Know that they know that which you have forgotten. Even those in grave circumstances and danger know this Truth.

Many have come to you through many means - the wind, a whistle, the sound of girls singing, a whisper in your dreams. They are all around you, calling you to listen so you can know what you have forgotten.

This is our sharing in words and music, for no word is without sound and all sound is a song. I am honored and overjoyed that you have chosen to read our words and hear our songs. Thank you for listening. Love YOU and you will love All."

AFTERWORD

There is one more gift we want to share with your children. As my life changed in the fall of 1998, my son was experiencing some scary dreams. To help and teach him, I chose to empower him at night with the knowing that he can choose how he will experience dreams. I began to share an affirmation with him each night just before he went to sleep. It is very powerful. Each night say it together or, as the parent, say it quietly for your children as they go to sleep.

This affirmation will open your children's hearts in joy. It is our gift to your children ... and you.

Affirmation of SelfLove

"I love me. I love the God-within that I am. I thank my Self for this wonderful journey of learning in joy. I ask the white light of protection to keep my bad dreams away and only let me have fun, funny, and happy dreams. I thank my body for being clear and healthy."

ACKNOWLEDGEMENTS

This book was not written and published without the participation of All. Many have lovingly shepherded it to you so that you can open your heart.

There are a few friends I would like to acknowledge by name because their effort, support, and love guided this book to your hands. I especially thank Marilyn Innerfeld, my friend, for all of her love and support in guiding me and editing this book. I want to thank Mahalakshmi Raja for her friendship, love and encouragement that I publish this book in print form so it can be shared. We share all that we are in joy and have found joy-beyond-joy within. Lastly, I thank the many readers who have shared with me how this book has touched their hearts.

ABOUT THE AUTHOR

Chris lives in the beautiful mountains of Colorado. She joyfully shares her life in love and friendship. She has chosen to share what she has learned with all who choose to understand what it means that we are God.

Her life completely changed when she experienced an extraordinary moment of discovery that awakened her heart to total knowing. She unexpectedly began to experience a "voice" and shortly thereafter to see souls across time. The experience of the "voice" and the messages of the souls shared powerful truths about love, abundance, life, hate, joy and creation. Moved by the breadth of the messages and the souls that shared with her she honored their call that she fulfill her life path in this lifetime—to walk the Earth as a messenger of the Simple Truth that we are all God.

In choosing to honor this path, she wrote both *The Simple Truth About God* and *Heart Songs: Messages for Parents from Children Across Time.* She came to know of her healing gifts—medical intuition, spiritual teaching and energetic healing as she worked with individuals and groups interested in understanding what it means to be God.

HEALING ARTS PUBLISHING

Healing Arts Publishing is dedicated to publishing books and materials that open hearts and minds to the Truth of our magnificence.

To learn more about our publications contact:

Healing Arts Publishing
P.O. Box 4223
Evergreen, CO 80437
303-674-7704

ChristineLenick@gmail.com
www.Facebook.com/ChristineLenick